Foun

For Custo

CW00449535

James Dodkins

Get a free company culture health check at
www.jamesdodkins.com/free-stuff

Foundations For Customer Centricity 2018
Copyright © 2017 by James Dodkins

Email: James.dodkins@bpgroup.org
Twitter: @JDodkins #Foundations
LinkedIn: uk.linkedin.com/in/jamesdodkins
Facebook: http://bit.ly/jamesdodkinsfb
Website: www.jamesdodkins.com
Blog: www.jamesdodkins.wordpress.com

Foreword

Anything great is built on solid foundations. That applies to buildings, the Coliseum, the Pyramids and the Taj Mahal. It applies to people, Martin Luther King, Mother Teresa and Nelson Mandela. This also applies to stories Cinderella, Lord of the Rings and Beauty and the Beast.

Stories are everything, they stir the emotions, they galvanise the spirit, they are a call to action. This book is all of that, helping us to see the obvious differently, helping us take immediate and tangible action to improve our lives, our work and our companies. If that inspires you then know you are not alone in the journey.

I take great pleasure in recommending to you a short, easy to digest and life changing story.

Foundations is THE business story of the 21st century.

- **Steve Towers, Founder and CEO, BP Group**

About the Author

As a teenager I played guitar in a heavy metal band, yes, that's right, I was a rock star. Jealous? Don't be, it's not all beer and women as some people would lead you to believe, there's a lot of carrying heavy stuff and sitting around…and being sweaty but in all honesty, I loved every second of it. We were signed, we released two albums and we toured the world, we were in magazines, had a video on TV and I even got to play alongside some of my idols, but unfortunately, like many things in life that we love, it imploded…spectacularly.

I now had a choice to make, after being an international rock god, what was my logical next step? Yes, you've guessed it, insurance. I joined an insurance company who because the fastest growing insurance company in UK history. I worked my way up the ranks and learned a lot, I loved it there, we were really helping people and making a difference, but unfortunately, like many things in life that we love, it imploded…spectacularly (can you spot a trend here?)

I struck out on my own and never looked back. Today I travel the world learning what the best performing companies on the planet are doing to succeed, their tools and techniques, their mindsets and attitudes, their tips and tricks. Then I come home, put all of that stuff into cool little methodologies, frameworks and systems, then travel the world some more teaching other companies how to replicate their successes. I've worked in 20 countries with over 400 companies and I like to think that I've made a difference along the way…that doesn't mean that I have…It just means that I like to think it.

Preface

*"If no one is criticising you,
you're doing something wrong"*

I'm just an ordinary guy with an extraordinary passion for customer experience and process improvement, for years I have been training and consulting with some of the biggest companies in the world working on BPM, Customer Experience and Process Improvement, Customer Centricity, Customer Strategy, and Company Culture projects. One problem that I always encountered was that people were determined to fit their new innovative ideas into their old, industrial age, out of date, hierarchical structures.

I would find that more often than not, after great work had been done that was consistently over achieving, things would slowly revert back to the way things were, some times even worse than before. If everything was better than before, why were people fighting to undo the good work that had been done? Why were people so committed to doing things in the old way?

It's been suggested by well meaning peers and colleagues (Including my mentor, BPM creator, Outside-In visionary, process legend and customer experience guru, Steve Towers) that I should write a book on the subject.

I have many goals in my life but being an author was never really one of them. Admittedly, I've written many published articles on various business subjects so I reasoned with myself that a book is just a collection of articles really. I don't possess the skills to become a brilliant business author, so I didn't set out to write a brilliant business books, plus I don't really like business books.

Reading business books has always been an aggravation for me, 400 pages later I'm left feeling a little cheated as the useful take-away information could have been distilled into one page. That's all I'll remember, that's all I'm going to use, anything else is just filler. If you go to GetAbstract.com you can get five-page summaries of thousands of books, each five-page summary is presented in a crisp magazine-page format. You can read it in less than 10 minutes, the perfect length to deliver the book's key ideas. The no-fluff summaries are logically structured to get the maximum out of your reading time. Services such as this wouldn't be able to exist if most books weren't crammed full of useless information to pad it out to an acceptable length.

This book is different, It's not going to be super-long, I'm not going to bore you with my entire life history, chances are you will have googled me and already know all about my story. I had a conversation with a very well known business book author and explained to them "It's probably only going to be like 100 pages long" I was told "Well you need to add some more in then don't you?" and in typical 'me' fashion I answered "Why? What a waste of time!" and the answer baffled me "Because that's what all the other business books are like, that's how everyone does it." Well as my school teachers would tell you "Because that's the way everyone else does it" has never been a good enough reason for me to do anything. Throughout my career I have worked in extremely fast paced, time sensitive, high-pressure environments. You had to get good at delivering a message as efficiently as possible and as far as your colleagues were concerned if you couldn't communicate it in one sentence you didn't know what you were trying to communicate and thus it didn't matter.

I have tried to only put in what is necessary for you to have a solid grasp of the philosophy and concepts and to be able to actually start making some changes, however due to the random tangent factory that is my brain I will undoubtedly end up going off point a lot, I'll try and edit out as many of those accidental detours as I can but some might slip through, sorry about that.

At points I'm going to refer to 'certain' companies rather than naming them. This is done for a very specific and particular reason. That reason is that I don't have permission and I don't want to get sued. A lot of the work I do is under Non Disclosure Agreement (NDA), I could have gone down the route of getting permissions etc but it would have taken a long time, and time is of the essence as I write this book. It could be that after I publish this book I will release a 'permission edition' with all the names, facts and figures after getting the go ahead from them…but I probably won't.

I've got no doubt that some people won't like this book, some purely because of the fact that it is short, some because of the viewpoints and opinions, others for the untraditional laid-back way the book has been written; well, if no one is criticising you, you're doing something wrong, right?

I'm glad the book is short, you can read it in an evening or on a flight and you won't be scared to read it again, a few times over. I hope that I start a revolution, where people only put what is really needed into a book and save us poor business people and all of those poor trees from a slow, boring, torturous death.

This book will not be for everyone; I am going to question the way people have been doing things for hundreds of years and suggest new ways of approaching business process and organisation, some people will find it scary and stop reading and disregard the ideas, others will find it inspiring and empowering and become advocates of the model. Either way, thank you for giving the book a chance to change how you think forever.

I felt the time is right to write this book as I've noticed that more and more industry experts are starting to talk about the ideas that you will read in this book, I don't know if they have heard me speak on the subject, if they have heard the ideas second hand or if they have stumbled across the ideas by themselves, either way none of them have quite got it right, so this book more than anything is to set the record straight, what I actually mean when I talk about organising your foundations for customer centricity.

Foundation *faʊnˈdeɪʃ(ə)n/*
noun: foundation; plural noun: foundations

An underlying basis or principle.
"this idea is the foundation of all modern economics"

The Oxford Dictionary of English, page 690

Introduction

"Their organisation's archaic structures were holding them back"

Around 5 Years ago I was starting to figure out the problem but was having real trouble explaining that what I knew in my head was the right way to go. It got to the point where in one meeting, where I was outlining the benefits of Outside-In thinking, trying to get a group of executives to understand that their organisation's archaic structures were holding them back and that before they could really change anything they needed to address this, that I hit a low point.

Why couldn't I find the words to help them see what I saw? That day I vowed to myself that I would crack it, I would take some time away to really nail what I believe to be the single biggest reason that most companies, no matter how hard they try, are not making the progress they deserve. Not just to help them but to help advance Outside-In thinking and Customer Centricity all over the world.

As you will learn throughout this book I rely on analogies quite a lot to explain what I'm trying to get across. I have never considered myself to be overwhelmingly articulate, so I set out to find the right analogy to convey my message.

Chapter One - What's Going Wrong?

"Just because you have a history doesn't mean you have a future"

Before we get into some of the right things to do let's look at some of the things people are doing wrong. The first thing we need to understand is that our customers are now very different animals. Both you and I as customers have transformed beyond recognition, our changing attitudes and habits make us very difficult to keep up with. Some people have described this phenomenon as the 'Enlightened Customer' and it takes an enlightened organisation to deliver outstanding service to this new breed.

The spread of the internet has been the catalyst for this change in customers, we are all connected to each other, we are connected all of the time without exception, we are connected through many different devices and mediums, we are living in an always-on world.

Because customers have been exposed to more of the world they can now chose to transact with more of the world; geographic location has never been less of a barrier. Customers now have access to a swathe of different options of who to do business with because they have been shown a new world of possibilities that just was not there before. Not only do customers have options of who to do business with, they are now barraged with a multitude of different options when doing business with them.

Take coffee for example; In the past our options were with or without milk and/or sugar and there was an unspoken understanding that the coffee would be hot. Today hearing the mind bending chimes of someone ordering an iced, half caff, ristretto, venti, 4-pump, extra shot, quarter foam, no cream, sugar free, cinnamon, caramel drizzle, dolce soy skinny latte...to go, is common place. We now live in a world where the people who serve us coffee need to be fluent in a minimum of 3 languages to even understand our orders, let alone the master's degree they need to make it.

Because of how the world is shaping up customers expectations are changing and evolving every single day, and now businesses have to keep up with these, customers expect more for less and quicker than ever before. Expectations are no longer industry specific; if a customer has a good experience with a tech company they forever wonder why they can't get that level of service with an airline.

There have been cases of 'Expectation Terrorism' where a rival company will hype up a competitors product before launch so much that when it finally launches, although a perfectly good product, it is distinctly underwhelming to all.

You will have heard the mantra "We need to exceed customers' expectations every time". In fact if you live by that you will fail and fast. As soon as you exceed an expectation that then becomes the expectation...and then what do you have to do? Yep, exceed it again. In this day and age for a customer to find a company who sets an expectation and then delivers on it nothing more, nothing less is a miracle.

Because of this inconsistent delivery on expectations companies have never been trusted less than they are today. Customers no longer believe what you say in your marketing messages and instead will take to the internet to find the opinions of their peers. In reality customers will now give more weight to the opinion of a perfect stranger than what you tell them about your product or service.

We all have a voice, no matter who you are, if you have access to the internet you will be heard and this is a nightmare for companies who are consistently delivering bad service, 20 years ago we were all told that if you gave a customer bad service they would go and tell 20 people. Today, if I receive bad service I tell 20 million people on twitter...in 20 seconds.

Practically all customers in the world today have an online voice and they particularly like the sound of it. Small blunders can turn into massive viral outrage, customers know this; they have become empowered to rebel like never before. Customers are becoming aware to the fact that the business is not doing them a favour by letting them use their product or service, the customer is doing the business a favour by choosing to do business with it.

Customers now have the ability to move between different companies at any given time for the slight mistreatment and taking into account that customers expectations are getting higher and higher every day, customer loyalty is becoming a very hard thing to come by. We refer to these customers as 'Promiscuous Customers'; a customer will go with anyone at any time to get what they want. We had done some work with a very large US credit card company, we asked them what their biggest problems are currently and the answer was astounding "Our biggest problem is our customers" they exclaimed. "Erm...OK...do explain" we urged, "Well, we give them an 12 month interest free credit card and do you know what they do after the interest free period runs out?" They asked, this was a rhetorical question as before any of us had time to put forward an answer it was given to us "They leave! Do they not know that it takes us 18 months to recoup the Return on Investment (ROI) of acquiring them?" They didn't like the answer "No, they don't know, and they wouldn't care if they did". Holding onto customers today is a lot harder than it used to be so taking a fresh approach is vital in any organisations survival.

Because customers now know they can move from company to company at the drop of a hat and that if things don't go well they can start an internet smear campaign, they have started to dictate the way in which companies transact with them. We refer to this as 'multi-channel experience'. For example, if I want to check my bank balance, I want to check it via SMS, on an app, on the internet, at an ATM, in a branch, by letter and by smoke signal. These are all capabilities that companies are having to build into their service yet having to keep prices the same because of the risk of losing customers, this is a very complicated and high pressure environment to operate within.

√hat's an Axolotl? Don't know? How would you find out? Yep, Google it. Within 30 seconds we can be quasi-experts in pretty much anything. Just incase you didn't Google it, its a weird fish/salamander thing that looks like a Pokémon. That's exactly what is happening now with customers and companies products and services.

Before most customers go to purchase anything they know exactly what they want, how they want it, how soon they want it and what Mary from Stockholm thought of it when she bought it. Customers have all become what some people refer to as 'Prosumers' - professional consumers. These prosumers are more connected and more well informed than any of your staff will ever be, gone are the days of customers trusting the sales person to have expert advice, many times the customer is now teaching the sales person.

Think of it this way, when was the last time you went to the doctors and didn't have a rough idea of what you were ill with because of the internet? I'm guessing you might not be able to remember. The majority of us now self diagnose and go to the doctor and tell them what we think we have, no longer do we go with symptoms and trust their professional opinion to connect the dots.

Because of how different customers are today, companies are trying very hard to give customers what they want. They will spend a lot of time and money on focus groups and surveys of how customers think they should run their business, what they could be doing differently and what else they could be offering, this is causing chaos.

The problem is that these companies think they are being customer centric, they are investing heavily both with time any money in these activities and finding that when they implement what they have found they are in a worse position than ever before. This then gives customer centricity a bad name, "We've tried that customer centricity stuff – it doesn't work" when in fact what they were doing was just about as far away from customer centricity than if they were to have done nothing at all.

Basing business decisions on what customers say that they want is a fast track, one way ticket to oblivion.

This is where 'Want vs. Need' comes into play. If you consistently deliver what customers say that they want, eventually you will fail however if you consistently deliver what the customer needs you will thrive.

We as customers are very good at telling people what we want and recently we have been sharpening these skills now that we have the internet as an open forum for other people to hear what we have to say. However, when it comes to articulating what we really need, we are awful.

Think of it like this, if you were to ask your children or a friend or relatives children tonight "What do you want to eat for dinner?" what kind of answers do you think you'd get? The answer might sound something like this "Gummy bears, chips, chocolate, cookies, burgers, ice cream…all on a pizza" however as adults we know what they need to eat to grow up strong and healthy and it is a very different proposition altogether.

Giving customers whatever they say that they want is like feeding children whatever they say that they want; expensive and unhealthy. We as business' need to understand what our customers need from us, even if they don't know it for themselves and work backwards towards the delivery of that real need, not what they have told us that they want. Always remember that as soon as you ask a customer what they want it creates an expectation that you will deliver it, don't set yourself up to fail.

That's why Voice of the Customer (VOC) exercises are a complete waste of time, they make people think they are being customer centric. Too many companies invest in the delivery of what customers have said that they wanted only to find out that by the time they deliver it, the customer wants something else or a competitor has delivered a need based solution that completely blows your offering out of the water.

Just think, while Nokia were busy researching and creating what their customers wanted, Apple were busy discovering and creating what customers really needed. None of us knew that we needed an iPhone before it was created, no amount of surveys, VOC projects or focus groups about what we want from a phone would have given us the ideas for a iPhone, I definitely didn't know I needed a smart phone before they existed but now I couldn't function without one.

Another problem business' are facing today is how they approach process and process improvement. Many people don't understand that process is just another name for the work that we do, everything an organisation does is process; there is not a single thing that isn't process and as a result a company's processes are its DNA. Traditionally when we have looked at process it has been through a functional specialist silo lens, focusing on departmental tasks and activities.

Most process improvement activities miss the most vital ingredient out…that's right, the customer. They hack and slash at the process without any thought as to how it will eventually effect the customer. We all need to wake up and realise that the sum of all of our process equals our customer's experience so to do any process work without a customer focus is suicide in the 21st century. In fact, a good strategy is to stop talking in terms of process all together and to only talk in terms of 'Customer Experience'.

Let's say that you already do the above right, there is an even bigger problem that many other companies face; the unwillingness to crumble what they have already created to make way for something new. Time and time again a business will realise that they have a process, a system or a department that is not needed any more and they find that it is actually standing in the way of progress and customer success. However, because they have spent time, money and energy on the creation of it they are unwilling to destroy it for the greater good. They are so focused on the past that they are blind to the future.

There is an overwhelming attitude that to get better in the 21st century you need to do what you did in the 20th century but better, quicker, more efficiently, for less money, with higher quality. Reality check, you can't meet the future by doing what you did in the past. It's not good enough to just get better at what you are already doing. As the saying goes, "just because you are doing things right doesn't mean that you are doing the right things" (Adapted from Deming). Many companies today are getting very smart and very clever at doing the wrong things really well and are paying their staff handsomely for the correct delivery of these wrong things.

It's like if I were to get a hammer and nail, and with one hand I were to place the nail in the little gap just behind my knee cap, and I were to raise the hammer up in my other hand and then strike the nail into my knee. I could have executed that process perfectly, maximum penetration, perfect angle and trajectory, flawless velocity…but no one ever stopped to point out that it's a really bloody stupid thing to be doing. We just go about doing what we are paid to do.

Lets say we were to try and improve the above process, chances are we would say "well, maybe if we had a bigger hammer, or a sharper nail that would remove any variation" "if we changed nail supplier maybe that would give us better nail quality" the I.T. guys would say "we could try using a nail gun to automate the process then you could put in a lot more nails in the same amount of time, or the same amount of nails with less staff, or maybe even move into other body parts". When what we really need to be asking is "Does this process really need to exist in the 21st century? Does this process contribute to the delivery of customer success and what the customer really needs?"

Currently there is a big problem with the methodologies that people are using for process improvement, most notable Lean and Six Sigma. Both are fantastic process improvement methodologies that were created to benefit a production process. People will dispute this but Lean and Six Sigma were not created to improve the customer experience; Lean and Six Sigma were not created to deal with the world as it is today. There are thousands of companies who have trained up their process teams in Lean and Six Sigma then have gone onto deploy the tools and techniques in a service environment, an environment that they were never created to be able to handle.

It's kind of like if when Henry Ford first started the production of the motorcar he took all of his wheel fitters and sent them on a horseshoe fitting training course. Very interesting and great for what it was created to do, but not relevant to fitting wheels in any way, shape or form.

Customer experience management is like a duck on a pond, the part you see above the water is the 'customer journey' and the legs under the surface are the internal processes and procedures. The legs are working away and drive the customer journey in a particular direction. Customers only see the above water portion of the duck and this duck can be in calm waters on a lovely sunny day or in choppy waters during a storm. Whether they know it or not the legs doing the work under the surface are deciding what direction the duck travels in, sunny or stormy but in business they are treated as separate things.

Internally our employees usually only see the legs. We work and work to make the legs move faster, more efficiently and more effectively but never come up to the surface to see in what direction they are steering the duck. In the real ducks world there is constant feedback and communication between the top and bottom of the duck making sure that the legs are propelling it in the right direction and if it isn't it makes changes as it goes to ensure success.

There are many different people who look to undertake customer experience and process improvement. The way they have been approaching these improvements is very, very wrong. Take Lean and Six Sigma for example, they focus on the legs, with emphasis on streamlining, improving and refining. They have no real understanding of whether the efforts will affect the duck in a positive or negative manner. 'Customer Journey' improvement projects only work on the body of the duck with no real understanding of what's driving the behaviour under the surface. The truly customer centric companies focus on the whole duck and treat customer experience improvement and process improvement as one and the same. They don't just map the body or the legs, they map it all and understand the relationship between internal work and customer touch points.

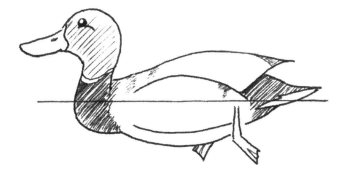

There are 3 types of company when it comes to customer experience; those who don't get it, those who think they get it and those who do get it. It's those who think that they get it that are the most damaging to the discipline.

Customer experience has been the hot topic around the board room for quite a while now, and we have all read about the successes of companies, big and small, that have been credited to their customer experience efforts. As a result of this, many companies have jumped into customer experience improvement projects without understanding the first thing about it; this has caused chaos. In the past, there were few companies who were doing customer experience very well that we could learn from, whereas today there is a swathe of companies who think they are doing customer experience well but who are actually falling flat on their faces. It's never been harder to find a good customer experience role model.

They spend their time doing customer surveys and focus groups because they think that customer experience is its own specialised function, they think that customer experience is all about marketing. They will say things like "we need to start doing customer experience"

Every company that has ever existed and every company that will ever exist has done and will 'do customer experience'; it is not a choice that you can make. The only choice you have is to take notice or not and just because you have not taken notice of it before doesn't mean that it hasn't existed.

Stop what you are doing and take a moment to try the following exercise.

Focus on your breathing, the flow of air in and out, the pace of it, the difference in temperature of your in and out breaths.

Focus on every time you swallow, the noise it creates in your ears, like a footstep on fresh snow.

Focus on your blinking, notice how you manually have to make yourself blink every single time. I hope you are still breathing.

Focus on that ringing sound in your ears, think about how constant it is, think about it's pitch.

Focus on how your seat feels, think about the pressure, the texture.

Focus on that itch, that itch that is somewhere on your body that you are now aware of.

Just because you have never focused on customer experience doesn't mean that it hasn't been there.

Because customer experience has been the number one buzz word for a while now, companies have engaged with large consultancies. They have been asking the question "Do you do this customer experience stuff? We need some help" and the big consultancies are not saying what they should be saying "Actually no we don't but there are many experts out there who can help you transform into a fully customer experience focused organisation" they are saying "…Urm…yeh sure…let me send over 100 consultants" and then they are delivering the same old work under the name of 'Customer Experience'.

The problem is executives with no guts. They are not buying consultancy work for results; they are buying it for excuses. Excuses for why they haven't hit targets; excuses for why they haven't achieved what they set our to do; excuses for why they are lagging behind the rest of the world. "It's not my fault, I hired in XYZ Consultancy" Nobody get's fired for hiring big blue. They would rather be safe than actually help the business progress and it is this mentality that is holding these companies back.

Maybe the biggest problem of all is technology. Not technology in itself but how people are using it. So many times we all see that technology is leading the business when it should be the exact opposite way. Technology is this elusive discipline that only the people who are smart enough can understand and anyone who is not in the club shouldn't get involved. That shouldn't be true of technology any more; technology is just todays pen and paper and should be as simple as that. People would never have said "Whoa there, you can't get involved in this project, you would never understand it, we're using really advanced pen and paper". Just look at the videos of tiny babies and 100+ year old people using tablets and smartphones because technology has never been more accessible. Both Steve Jobs and Jeff Bezos, two of our lifetimes greatest customer centric leaders, have said time and time again that we need to start with the customer experience and work backwards towards the technology, not the other way round. Customer experience should always decide the technology and never be decided by it.

Chapter Two - Traditional Structures

"Everything you have done in business until now has been created on the assumption that the org chart exists. It is never questioned, only obeyed."

If you think about your organisation's structure, what shape comes to mind? It is most likely a pyramid. The CEO sits at the top and everyone else cascades outwards below them. This diagram is knows as an 'organogram', you may know it by its more common name as an 'org chart'.

Let me set the scene and take you back to the year 1776 to a small Pin Factory in Scotland and a man you will most likely have heard of: Adam Smith. Adam Smith was a social philosopher and a pioneer of political economy and on the 9th of March, 1776 he published the book that has formed how we do business to this very day, this book was called 'The Wealth of Nations'.

Adam Smith had looked into the inner workings of the aforementioned Scottish pin factory and noticed some extraordinary things; one being that the pin factory's productivity was largely dependent on what employee was present at work on any given day and the level of their skill set. He also noticed that there were 18 discrete tasks that took place to produce a pin. Smith looked deeper into the workings of the pin factory and created what is described as the 'division of labour' (and later the subdivision of labour) where individual tasks were clearly defined and each person was assigned, trained and closely managed to effectively complete their task. This revolutionised manufacture and production; he increased productivity reportedly by 24000% and his teachings were cited in the declaration of independence as the US model for economic growth.

This was a complete shift from the traditional way of production at the time, where one man would own and complete every step of the creation from start to finish. This required a great deal of skill from the craftsmen whereas with the division of labour the worker only had to know how to complete their one task proficiently, they had no need to know of any other steps in the process.

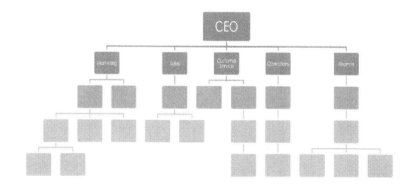

The pyramidal, hierarchical, functional specialism org. chart that we use today came out of this work. Each person has a task or tasks to do and they get trained and rewarded to complete those tasks very well. They have someone above them who manages, guides and controls what they do, who in turn has someone above them who manages, guides and controls their work all the way to the top where the CEO sits. We have all organised ourselves as if we were a 1776 pin factory.

Lets look at what has happened in the world since 1776. The world's first steam locomotive journey, the world's first photograph was taken, Morse Code was invented, the refrigerator, the telephone and the light bulb were all invented. The world's first airplane flight , television, nuclear power, PC's and laptops all came into existence. The internet, CD-ROM's, DVD's, USB storage devices, smartphones and tablets were all invented after the creation of the organogram in 1776. If we were to bring Adam Smith forward in a time machine (currently not invented) to the world today he would be astounded by how much things have changed. Chances are he would ask us the inevitable question "This world you now live in is so vastly different to that of 1776, pray tell, how do you now organise yourselves and the work that you do?" and unfortunately we would have to answer "Well, Mr. Smith, we liked the work that you did with the pin factory so much that we still run things exactly like that today". What do you think his reaction to that would be? Exactly, he would think we were insane, and he would have a point. Every single thing on this planet has changed dramatically in over 200 years apart from how we organise ourselves and the work that we do.

Some people take exception to me suggesting that everything has stayed the same, of course there have been many advancements in many different areas; communications, data handling, customer service tools, process improvement methodologies the list goes on but I would still argue that nothing has really changed. Imagine if my wife and I built a small house to live in together and we built it to perfectly suit our needs. Then the years pass and we get a pet, and have children, and then an elderly relative comes to stay for a while and one day my wife turns to me and says "This house that we built many years ago, although perfect for our past needs, just doesn't have the capabilities to cope with the needs of today, we need to change" and I reply "No problem, leave it to me".

Now let's imagine that I went to the local hardware store and bought the biggest, most expensive, most technologically advanced pot of red paint that was available anywhere in the world. Let's imagine that I take this paint home and paint every single one of the walls in the house with it. When my wife gets home she looks around in shock and cries "What have you done?" then I reply "I've changed everything, look how different everything is, there isn't a single thing that looks the same as before!"

This is exactly what we have done in business, instead of changing the foundations that were created in 1776 to a 21ˢᵗ century model. Instead of changing the foundation that underpins, forms and constrains every piece of work that we do. Instead of changing the foundations that were created to help a pin factory run more effectively to something more appropriate to our 'age of the customer' service environment, all we have done is paint the walls, over and over again.

The org chart that is your company's foundation was not designed to deliver exceptional customer experience in the 21st century and no amount of wall painting will ever change that.

Usually at this point, whether I'm talking with one person, to a board room full of people or to a packed out auditorium, I will find a picture on the wall, on someone's note book, or I will draw a picture on a flip chart (If I have to draw it myself it's usually a tree). I will then point to the drawing and ask the other person or people "What is this?" Without fail I am always met with the chorus of "It's a tree!" to which they are met with the echoes of "Wrong answer, try again" to which I am in return met with confused faces.

I then go on to explain that the correct answer is "A picture of a tree". You cannot touch this tree, you cannot climb this tree, you cannot carve your name into it, it doesn't produce oxygen, it doesn't produce fruit, you cannot make any products from it, wildlife cannot live in it, it will never seed new trees and it will never grow and will never die because this tree does not exist, all that exists is a picture of a tree.

In direct parallel, your org chart doesn't exist, all that exists is a drawing of an org chart, yet we treat it as if it is a living breathing physical thing. Think about every aspect of the work that you do today, it is all formed, shaped and controlled by a drawing.

We talk about the org chart as if it is a physical entity, we talk about silo walls as if they actually exist, we talk about climbing the ladder as if it actually exists, we talk about chain of command as if it actually exists. None of these things actually, physically exist. It is a collective hallucination.

Every system you have ever used, every process improvement methodology, every management model, everything you have done in business until now has been created on the assumption that the org chart exists. It is never questioned, only obeyed. Departments, internal customers, silo walls, managers, service level agreements (SLA), chains of command, targets, divisions, service process, value streams and so on don't actually exist, they are just a construct of the mind. They only exist because of the way we draw the chart; if we drew the chart in a different way none of these would exist. It is an abstract illusion. If we were to stop thinking about a table or a chair, they would still exist, if we were to stop thinking about departments and hierarchies they would not. The only reason they still exist is because we continue to think of them as real.

This method of drawing an organisational diagram has created a Rubik's Cube out of our companies, each where colour represents a department. Everybody is assigned their colour and then given tasks and activities that are in the interest of that colour's success. They are trained and coached to do the best work in the interest of their colour. They are then targeted and given bonuses on the success of their colour. However, because we are all so focused on the success of our colour we wouldn't think twice before screwing up other colours work to further our colours success.

This has created an internal battle ground where we are all very focused on out doing and competing against other departments and as a result have very little trust left within our organisations. Remember that the pyramid is a control structure to make sure you complete your task or tasks proficiently; it is not a support structure created to help deliver fantastic customer experience.

What this has meant is that today's employees are more bothered about the success of their department and hitting targets than they are about the customer experience. They get passed messages and company edicts about the customer and the customer experience but are still targeted and rewarded on the success of their department. They all have a dose of 'The customer isn't my job syndrome'. You might be sitting there thinking, "Well, the customer *isn't* everyone's job" but remember; the only reason that we think like that is because of the way we draw the diagram. It doesn't matter how innovative and well created your customer experience may be, if it is then forced to operate within an archaic control structure, you will fail. You can't fire a bullet with a bow.

Where as the pyramidal org chart caused great success in the past, however today it is causing pandemonium. Remember, the org chart was created to bring order and control to a factory setting so when we apply this to the 21st century, service heavy environment it causes us to do some very odd things and do work in some very odd ways.

Today it's all about showing the guy or gal at the top of the pyramid that you are doing a good job and that you shouldn't be fired. You show your boss how well you are doing, who in turn shows his or her boss and so on all the way to the top. There is no actual guarantee that you are genuinely doing a good job but as long as you can make it look like you are, you are safe.

What this causes is business decisions made by the CEO based on faulty data. In the pin factory the CEO was the person who knew the most about pin making so he could effectively guide the organisation to pin making success. Ask yourself the question, and answer it as honestly as you can, does your CEO know the most about your business? (or if you are the CEO do you know the most?) 99.9% of the time the answer will be a big fat "NO". Yet, this is the person making the decisions on behalf of the business, how does that make sense? The only reason it is done this way is because of the 1776 pin factory model, not a 21st century customer age model.

Some companies have approached this problem and found what they think to be more appropriate representations for the 21st century, A flat or horizontal chart represents individuals along the same level, not identifying greater standing to an individual's title by placing them higher than any other individual. A matrix structure has added complexity, with individuals clustered by their collective skill sets but also by the groups in which they work and superiors they may report to. These are still just variations on the same theme and have one very vital element missing.

In the 21st century, the 'Age of the customer', what is the one big thing missing from the 1776 org chart and its variations? That's right, the customer! How can any company claim to be a customer centric organisation without the customer even on the map?

 The more advanced companies in the 21st century have been known to draw the org chart with the customer in the middle and everything else orbiting the customer. Some organisations have been known to keep the pyramid but have the customer at the very top clearly showing every one in the company that the customer is everyone's boss, some people put the customer either end of the model and say that this denotes end to end process. The issue with these is that many of them are still departmentally segregated and in siloes. In this book I will share the most appropriate way to approach this diagram in the 21st century; it will still be just a drawing however it's a more suitable drawing for this day and age.

Chapter Three - Questions That We Need To Ask

"Don't segment by circumstance, categorise by need"

Before dramatically changing anything there are always questions we need to ask ourselves about our customers, our process and our employees.

"When we say process, what do we mean?" When we talk about process we need to be thinking in terms of customer experience, not just the internal work. When you look at process without the customer experience you are only ever dealing with effects. Every piece of work that you do can be traced back to a customer interaction, so you need to be aware of it when looking at process. Don't just make the effect better, fix the cause. If I were to go to the doctors because I was having chest pains and the doctor examined me and said "Well, you have come to me complaining of chest pains, so to fix that I will prescribe aspirin to make the pain go away" I would be looking for a new doctor quickly to find out what the real cause of the pain was. So many times in business, people have been looking at process in the wrong way we have just been engineering the effects, we need to change the mindsets so that we engineer at the causal level.

"Who is the customer?" Before any process improvement project begins you need to know who you are making it better for, not just that you are making it better. I would always suggest that this should be an external customer, not an internal customer. Technically internal customers don't exist but if external customers are unavailable then you have to start where you are. Even if you are improving a process for an internal customer you really need to understand their needs inside and out.

We shouldn't be looking at customer segments, we should be looking at customers that have been categorised by need. When we segment customers it is by circumstance, age, geographic location, income, core, high potential, high value; we have no insight into who these customers really are and what their needs are. When you categorise customers by need you will group customers together that would never have been in the same group before if you had used a segmentation exercise. Designing process for customer categories allows you to deliver their needs rather than delivering a one-size-fits-none standardisation model.

Not everyone is your customer. We have been taught throughout our entire business lives to get as many customers as we can and then hold onto them for dear life. It's kind of like mining for diamonds but instead of sorting the rocks from the gems you just cut and polish them all. The best strategy is to define the customers that you want, go out and get them and deliver amazing customer experience to them. When 'everyone' is our customer we deliver a weak standardised process to try and cover all bases and it means that everyone gets an over inflated, convoluted process instead of a laser focused experience based on specific categories needs. You will tend to find that 20% of your customers cause 80% of your costs, get rid of them…fast! Stop buffing the rocks when you should be polishing the diamonds.

Various government organisations have said to me "Yes, I see what you are saying however, really, everyone is our customer" Where as that might be true...ish, it's very rarely accurate. For everyone to be your customer you would literally need to be serving every person on the planet. If the World Health Organisation said that everyone in the world is their customer I'd agree but most of the time you will not be in the same situation. Even then, it doesn't mean that you have to treat everyone the same. You can still categorise them and treat them in very different ways depending on their needs and SCO.

"Where does the process really start and finish?" When I catch a flight the process doesn't start from the moment I buy a ticket and it doesn't end when I collect my baggage. When you analyse customer experience as the process, the start and finish points shift dramatically. For me it starts when I become aware of the trip I need to take and it ends when I'm home again afterwards. When you start to look at the customer experience as the process you get a very different view of how the world works, not just a departmental silo based interpretation. When looking at customer experience one of the most vital aspects that needs to be understood is that there is a lot of experience that happens before and after their first and last interaction with you as a company. To ignore that doesn't mean that it doesn't happen, it just means that you have no control over it.

"What business are we really in?" Most companies today have become caught in a trap. These companies are defining the business they are in by what they do, not by what outcome they are there to achieve. For example there is a certain German company that makes cars, however they are not in the automotive business, they are in the business of 'Joy'. Yes they make automobiles, that's what they do but they define themselves by what they look to deliver to their customers. Don't fall into the trap of "yes that's a great idea but an airline would never do that" or "we have to have this in there because it's an insurance industry standard". You need to redefine what business you are in to really be able to innovate. Once you have redefined the business you are in you can benchmark against other people who deliver that outcome well, not just against other people who do the same things. Just like how the Apple stores benchmark against Ritz-Carlton Hotels.

For example; I recently worked with a wealth management division of a certain large American financial institution who were looking at how to attract more customers. When they were asked what business they are in they replied with "Wealth Management" to which I replied "Wrong answer, try again" to which I was in return met with confused faces. I explained that wealth management is what they do and not what business they are in.

I then asked them what the outcome is that they are there to achieve for their customers. After much to-ing and fro-ing they decided that they are actually in the business of "Financial Freedom" and that this is the outcome their customers really need from them. They then looked at other companies whose customers were seeking financial freedom and we came across the idea that people use online casinos to find financial freedom (although it very rarely concludes that way). One way that online casinos draw new people in is to offer their first bet risk free, if the customer wins they keep the winnings but if they loose the company refunds the bet. The idea that came out of this was to allow customers to invest certain amounts of money risk free for 6 months and if their portfolio grew they kept the money and could reinvest but if it had lost money for any reason the company would refund the loss. It is a fantastic way to get more customers involved in wealth management that they would not have thought of if they had not redefined what business they were in.

"What are the customers expectations?" Expectations are a largely overlooked area of process and customer experience. Our expectations are being formed and evolved everyday by every different company and product that we come into contact with. We need to see what the customer's expectations are from this process then meet or exceed them. Earlier I said that exceeding customers expectations can be a bad thing, but only if you aim to exceed them at every single interaction.

Re-setting an expectation is great, however you need to make sure you can consistently deliver on it time and time again, if you can't then you need to see what needs to change: how you do things or the customers expectation. Don't confuse asking a customer their expectations with asking them what they want. They are very separate things. When I check my bank account: I expect the ATM to be working, I want there to be £1 Billion pounds in my account. One of those the company can deliver on, the other might be a little bit harder.

"Are we trying to deliver what customers have told us they want, or have we figured out what they need?" We have already covered the difference between need and want and by delivering what the customer needs over what they say that they want you will always be one step ahead. This is also true when it comes to offering options. If you need to offer your customers options, you don't know what your customer needs. I will clarify this as there are some exceptions.

If one of your customers needs is to have options then the above statement becomes void, for example, the type of customers who were to buy a Rolls Royce have 'options and configuration' as a core need. A real need to personalise the vehicle to represent them and their status. In any other situation giving a customer options is tantamount to asking them 'what do you want?' Really think about it, if you already knew exactly what your customer needed you wouldn't need to give them options.

Now, the technology and insight to be able to run a completely option-less company might be a way off but there are ways and means of getting close in this day and age. To start with, before you have customer categories using options to determine the categories is a good start; profile the customers and their choices so you can start to understand how certain customers act and personalise their experience based on this information so you can start to offer fewer options. Once you really understand your customers needs you can offer less and less options.

A certain South Korean car company has realised that offering options lengthens the process, thus creating greater dissatisfaction and actually costing more to administer the process. They have concluded that it is far more cost effective to offer every single car fully loaded, no more 'optional extras' as every car has everything. This costs them a hell of a lot less because they don't need different production tracks, different ordering systems, different pricing structures.

The customers are happier because they know that even though they are paying the same price they are getting everything included and it means that their cars are produced quicker and delivered faster. Revenues are higher because people are going to the company that gives everything over the company that makes you chose and pay more. This was only possible because they understood their categories of customer extremely well. For example this would not fly with a Rolls Royce customer.

vv nat is the Successful Customer Outcome?" How can you redesign a process if you don't know the outcome you are looking to achieve? For the customer in this process, what does a successful outcome look like? You must fully understand the Successful Customer Outcome (SCO) that needs to be delivered and make sure that everything you do is aligned towards the delivery of it. Most of the time it will be in line with the business that you are really in.

If we take the German automotive company again they will ask themselves "For this category of customer, in this process, what does 'Joy' look like to them?" and they will make sure that every single task and activity is aligned towards the delivery of the answer.

You can then create customer outcome based process metrics. I refer to these as Key Outcome Indicators (KOI's) they are the measurable targets that directly link towards the delivery of the SCO. The great thing about KOI's is that they have yes or no answers. Did we deliver this? Yes or No. Every single person in the process is targeted and rewarded on the delivery of these KOI's regardless of department or status. You can imagine how different the work environment is when all of a sudden the customer is everyone's job.

"Is everyone in the new process being rewarded for the delivery of customer success?" In reference to the KOI's above, you don't want to create a fantastic new process only to have it slowly revert back to the way it was because the reward systems are still departmentally focused, everyone in a process no matter what department should be targeted and rewarded on the delivery of customer success. Then all of a sudden everyone is working together to make the customer happy instead of against each other to help their department 'win'. Outcome based rewards give employees the empowerment to do whatever it takes to deliver.

Chapter Four - Built Around Outcomes, The Football Team Analogy

"If we look at the departmental mentality of business, people are targeted and paid for completing tasks and activities that are department specific"

If you remember back to the situation that I told you about at the beginning of the book where I was looking for an analogy to explain to a group of executives, in no uncertain terms, just how they needed to look at things? Well this is it.

In the 21st century, to be able to deliver an outstanding customer experience every single time, you need to change the foundations of your business. Your entire business is built on top of your method or organisation, so it has to change.

You need to organise yourself like a football (or soccer if you are an American) team. Let's look at a football team and ask ourselves the most important questions from the previous chapter.

Who is the customer? This is usually a very obvious answer however I do sometimes get some difference of opinion, some people think that the manager and coach are the customer, some people think that the club owner is the customer, some people have said that the ball is the customer (I don't really understand that one), however I think we can all agree that for a football team it is the fans who are the customer.

What is the successful customer outcome? For a fan who has travelled to see their team play, what does success look like for them? Again, I think we can all agree that 'winning the game' is the ultimate successful outcome for the fan.

So what would be the best way for a football team to organise a team to achieve this? Would we put all of the defenders out to play the game? And then put all of the strikers out to play the game? And then put all of the goal keepers out to play the game? No, but why do we do this in our companies?

We put all of the I.T. guys together, we put all of the customer service guys together, we put all of the sales guys together into different departments.

What a football team has is a clear vision of the outcome it needs to deliver, and as a result put a team together with a mix of different skills and specialisms who are best suited and most likely to deliver the win.

Remember this will be a team made up of goal keepers, defenders, midfielders and strikers, within each skill set there will be different specialisms, long balls, holding play, free kicks, crossing and so on; every member of the team will be very different to the next but what they all have in common is that they know they are there to get the win.

Now if we look at the departmental mentality of business, people are targeted and paid for completing tasks and activities that are department specific; vary rarely for delivering outcomes. If we were to try that on the football field things would get very strange very quickly. Imagine that you were a defender and you weren't targeted on getting the win, let's say you were not bothered about the win at all, instead you were targeted and rewarded on making at least 4 tackles and 50 complete passes per game, chances are you would pass the ball about between your fellow defenders to get your pass rate up and rejoice when the opposition were attacking as it gave you a chance to get your tackle rate up, you might even pass the ball to the opposition to give you the chance to tackle. That is in no way good for the team as a whole and is no way going to help deliver the win for the fans.

In our organisations, we are also very territorial, we only do things for our departments and get very protective as soon as another department tries to get involved and in turn face hostility if we dare to stray into another department. If we encounter work that isn't to do with our department we pass it off to the 'correct' department. Imagine if a football team were to behave like that. Let's imagine that we are a striker in the last minute of the world cup final and we see that an opposition striker is about to run into open space and most likely score for the winning goal. If we took this mentality we would run up to this player and say to them "Excuse me, you need to be tackled by one of our team. I'm a striker so I only take shots and score goals, you need a defender to tackle you, as a striker I'm not qualified to do that. Can you wait there please while I transfer you to a defender who can tackle you?" That would just not work.

When you put a team together with different specialisms they will perform different roles in the process because they have a clear team vision of the outcome that they need to achieve. They become empowered to do whatever it takes to deliver that outcome; strikers will tackle, defenders will run with the ball up the field, there have even been times when the goal keeper has scored a goal for his team.

This doesn't mean that the amount of tackles, the amount of yards run, the amount of saves made and the amount of shots on target aren't important; it's just that they are no longer the most important metric of success. So, what is? The final score. Everyone should be targeted and rewarded on that outcome not the tasks and activities that lead up to it.

Why don't we do this in our business'? Because of how the org chart has caused us to do work. As long as you know who the customer of the process is and what their successful customer outcome is, you can set to work at putting mixed specialism teams together that are best suited to it's delivery.

There are other parallels too, for instance if we take the referee. The referee is the equivalent to the regulator and too many times the regulator is considered as the customer. Companies gear everything they do towards making the regulator happy as if that is the end goal. The customer gets forgotten about and receives shoddy service. It doesn't really matter how happy the regulator is if you have no customers left.

In football it is all about getting the win while keeping the referee happy, keeping the referee happy isn't the win in itself. You would never hear the coach during the half time team talk saying "Guys! Great game, fantastic work, yes, we're losing 6-0 but we haven't picked up a single red or yellow card or made any fouls...keep up the good work"

It's not like they have to send all of their players on training courses and introduce team wide standards and controls so that the players don't commit hand ball offenses; they know that in order to achieve the win it is a pre-requisite that you need to commit the least amount of fouls possible. It is exactly the same in the more progressive 21st century companies, even in heavily regulated environments. They know the outcome they need to achieve and it is a pre-requisite that certain regulations have to be met and adhered to in order to be able to deliver that outcome successfully. Not that the success is the compliance to the regulation.

In organisations there is very little trust, mainly because of the way we organise things. You have a job to do and your boss' job is to make sure that you are doing it right and so on. This makes employees feel like they cannot be trusted and in return they give very little trust back. Whenever anything goes wrong, rather than just getting on with things and making it better we all play the blame game of why our boss should be angry at anyone apart from us. Trust is virtually non-existent between us in our organisations. Even if you have a good department where trust is very strong, you don't trust the other departments because they are most of the time seen as competitors.

In a football team you all work together to achieve a shared objective so you naturally foster a trusting culture within the team; trust that the players will fill their roles, trust that if you need help there will be another player there to assist you, trust that if you mess up you have other team mates that will help put things right, not just wait for you to fail then point and blame. There is no "Well I made lots of good tackles so the loss isn't my fault". They play as a team, win as a team and lose as a team and the fans love it.

This creates fan loyalty, the fans can see that each and every member of the team is working as hard as they can, doing whatever it takes to get the win, not just passing the buck until someone other than them has to do more work or gets the blame. Fan loyalty has never really been much of an issue for football teams or any sports teams for that matter. This is exactly the same with customers, even if you don't achieve the outcome, even if you mess up, if customers can see and feel that everybody at every point cared and was trying to do the right thing they become very forgiving. Loyalty is one of the hardest things for companies to come by in this day and age because of the amount of choice available. There are companies that have cult like loyalty behind them and it comes from this type of approach.

When it comes to football there is very little standardisation; teams will run standardised set pieces from corners and free kicks, and may have certain procedures for defending and attacking but as a whole the players have the freedom to do whatever it takes to deliver the win. It's not a case of you need to make 14 passes as a team before you can take a shot because that is best practice, or you need to run at least 20 yards with the ball before you can pass it to another player because that meets an ISO standard. You would never hear a coach saying "Yes that was a fantastic game and a brilliant win! However you didn't hit your pass rate target, try harder next time."

In business we are obsessed with standardising everything, however customer experience isn't standard, we are all different and we experience everything differently every single time, so trying to force us into a standard, one size fits all approach will undoubtedly lead to a poor experience for all. When a team really understands what the outcome is that they are there to achieve there is no need to standardise anymore. On average 20% of a process on average can be standard, the rest should be flexible dependent on who you are dealing with and the outcome that they need to achieve, remember different customers may have different SCO's from the same process, you can't cater to that if you standardise everything.

In a business you fit into one of three tiers, you are either the customer, an employee or support staff. Every employee's job is to deliver the SCO, every support staff's job is to aid other employees in the SCO delivery therefore everything you do should be aligned to delivering customer success. Just getting people to think this way will dramatically change how you do work.

In a football team there are trainers, club doctors, physiotherapists, cleaners, dieticians, psychologists, grounds keepers and so on and it is their job to make sure that the team are in the best possible position to achieve the win. Every single person within the club knows the end objective and therefore everything they do is in the benefit of it's delivery.

In a football team the real stars, the ones that get the most recognition and the highest pay are the players, the ones actually out there doing the customer facing work, not the executive team. This is the opposite in traditional business, the employees that actually do the customer facing work are the lowest on the pyramid and get paid the least whereas the executives and the CEO get paid the most and get all of the acknowledgement. Why is this? Because of how we draw and think about the diagram.

An interesting question to ask yourself is: Where do Executives and CEO's fit in this three tiered approach? Well as they aren't directly part of the customer experience, and they aren't the customer then they become support staff and it is now their job to make life easier for everyone else. CEO's should be serving the employees, not the other way round.

I'm actually a very big advocate of CEO-less companies, like DPR Construction. DPR don't even have job titles on their business cards for it's employees as their co-founder Doug Woods (who funnily enough if you do enough googling is listed as their CEO) believes that "when you start putting labels on employees, it puts restrictions on what employees think they can do and on what others think they can do."

I'm not saying that every company should be CEO-less, I'm just saying that for some companies it is the right choice. Many companies have tried to go CEO-less in the past and failed but unless you have your foundations right first it is never going to work. There will always be companies that need CEO's and there will always be companies who would be better off without them. Maybe it depends on if you have the right CEO or not. It's better to have no CEO than the wrong CEO.

Going CEO-less is a very interesting topic that garners a multitude of different opinions and emotions. However I don't want to go too far off track, maybe it's a good subject for another book?

If you think about a process or customer experience in your own organisation now, think about who that customer really is and the outcome that they need to receive from interacting with you. What specialties would be needed in the team that was best suited to deliver it? Marketing? Sales? Customer service? Finance? Just imagine if you could put a team together to specifically deliver that outcome and they were all rewarded on the outcomes delivery not for completing tasks and activities. Imagine how the work dynamic would change from being an inwardly focused department oriented environment to a truly customer centric ecosystem. This will cost you far less money to administer and will achieve a far superior customer experience, in return generating higher revenues. That's the Holy Grail...or the World Cup if you will.

Chapter Five - The Organisphere

"You can't meet the future by doing what you did in the past"

Essentially there are two job roles in an organisation, I refer to them as circles. You have the 'Customer Experience Circle' (CXC), known as the 'Inner Circle' and the Employee Support Circle (ESC), known as the 'Outer Circle'. The inner circle contains the employees that are actively involved in delivering your customer experience, every one else is now effectively thought of as having a support role. The closer you are to the customer the greater your influence is over the customer experience is. No matter how well the experience is designed, no matter how good your policies are, no matter how good your reward system is, at the end of the day the people who deliver the experience hold the most influence as to how it runs and are arguably the most important employees in the organisation.

Gartner reported that "A single contact center with 200 agents engages in an average of 10,000 hours of interactions with customers per week" Think about it, that is likely your lowest paid, least valued and least invested in employees delivering over half a million hours of customer experience per year, you think the guys at the top of the pyramid have the most influence over the success of your company? Think again!

Many of you and many of the people that you tell about this will not really like that premise. As someone who climbed the corporate ladder, I get it. To be told that the first job role you had holds more influence in the 21st century than the job role you have worked 10-15 years to get really sticks in your throat.

As an aside, 'climbing the corporate ladder' is another analogy that we use that further embeds the idea that the organisation pyramid is a physical structure not the mental construct that it actually is.

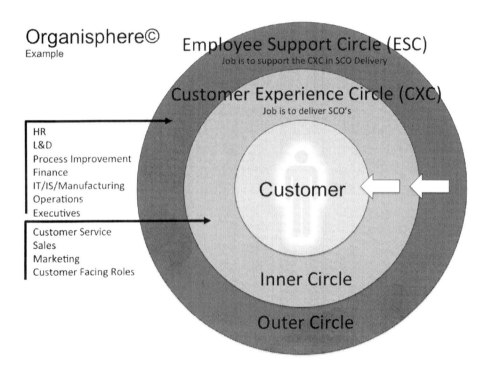

Back to the point I was trying to make. It's just like in football, the inner circle contains the players, the ones who day in day out have the final responsibility of delivering the customer experience. Every one else is only there to help make that run smoothly, they are the outer circle. Simple really isn't it?

This is a very visual way of showing everyone in the organisation how everything they do is aligned towards the delivery of success to customers. No more departments, just people whose job it is to deliver successful customer outcomes and people whose job it is to support them, no more, no less.

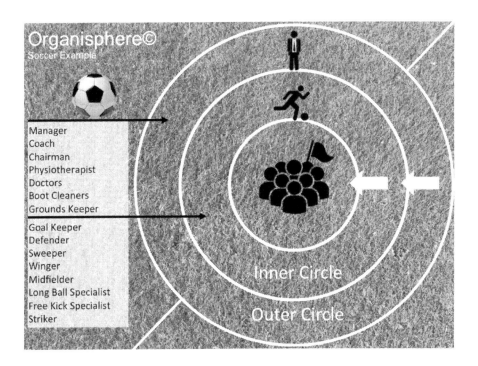

Organisphere©
Soccer Example

Manager
Coach
Chairman
Physiotherapist
Doctors
Boot Cleaners
Grounds Keeper

Goal Keeper
Defender
Sweeper
Winger
Midfielder
Long Ball Specialist
Free Kick Specialist
Striker

Inner Circle

Outer Circle

Within the Organisphere we don't have departments but we do have 'Experience Teams' and these teams aren't static, one employee could be part of many experience teams. We start to phase out the talk of process and only talk about experience. We start to realise what we used to think of as process is usually just a tiny part of an entire customer experience and an entire customer experience will touch multiple processes across the organisation.

Each customer experience has a team and in this team the members have different specialties, these specialties are decided by what skills are needed to deliver a successful customer outcome for that experience. You end up with a multi skilled team who are learning from each other everyday how to better deliver SCO's with the least number of handoffs possible.

If you don't know how to do something you pass the customer to someone who does and stay around so you know a little bit more next time around. Something that couldn't be done within our old hierarchical structures but something that is very fast and simple to do within Experience Teams.

Welcome to your new org chart, it may look like the blue prints to a spaceship, but this is your new foundation for customer centricity. Each set of concentric circles is a possible experience in the customer lifecycle and the straight lines represent their relationship to each other. From Buying the product or service, using it, queries regarding it, complaints, retention etc etc. It's all there. Remember these teams are put together for their ability to deliver customer success in any given experience and may appear in more than on experience.

New org chart

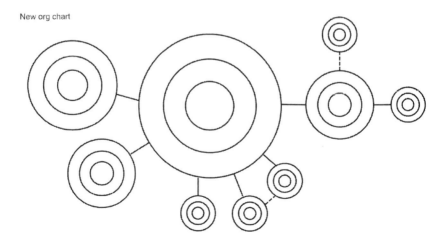

Chapter Six - Measurements

"It is your own fault if you can't trust your employees, you have obviously hired the wrong people."

I've already mentioned that in a truly customer centric company the employees will be rewarded for the delivery of successful customer outcomes, that should make perfect sense by now. You should be rewarding for the achievement of outcomes not measurements of tasks and activities.

Now you might be thinking that this will require a great deal of change management and many years of migration to this radical new way of doing things. You couldn't be further from the truth.

As soon as you link what you want to achieve (customer success) with what your employees want to achieve (their pay check) your change management is done. If you went to any employee and said, "Your bonus is now solely dependent on you delivering a successful customer outcome" What do you think the first question will be? "What is the successful customer outcome?" Change management done.

Now you will understand that that is a very simplified version of how things will actually run and maybe I should point out that the money isn't the sole driver for many employees. For many employees recognition, personal investment, empowerment and a sense of being trusted are big drivers too.

Now remember the deal is that the employee's bonus is dependent on achieving the SCO, not necessarily on how they do it. In a truly customer centric organisation the employee will be empowered to do whatever it takes and work with whoever they need to work with in order to make the right things happen for the customer. This demonstrates a massive level of trust in your employees, just like a football manager has to trust that his players will do the right thing to get the win.

It's also amazing how smart people become when you empower them to make their own decisions. Remember, in a football team, the players don't have to formally request to do something that is outside of their core competency; if they think it will contribute towards success, they will do it. It is exactly the same when we move to this truly customer centric model, managers aren't there to make all of the decisions, they are there to help make sure the employees are in a position where they can make the right decisions for themselves. Steve Towers calls this "Action in the moment" capability. Anyone in the organisation is able to make a decision on behalf of the company at any time.

This might be a little bit scary, you might be thinking "In theory this sounds great, but we could never trust our employees to do this". First of all, why do you expect your employees to trust you when you don't trust them? Why don't you trust them? Because you haven't been recruiting for customer success you have been recruiting for task completion and departmental success. It is your own fault if you can't trust your employees, you have obviously hired the wrong people.

You will notice that very passionate, normally very expressive people come to work and get told to keep their head down and just do what they are told; and basically get forced into a box and held back from their full potential. Don't think, do. This is not the right environment to breed a happy, healthy employee, the type of employee that will deliver the best experiences to your customers. An environment of trust and support will undoubtedly turn your organisation into a fantastic place for your customer to do business with but also an amazing place for people to work.

How do we create these measures? Well remember there will be different types of customers based on need and they should all be treated differently, no more standardisation. Firstly, it is very important to understand who the customer is and what their expectations are. Then based on the experience you can use this very simple template to create your Key Outcome Indicators (KOI's) the target that everyone in the experience will be trying to achieve no matter of specialty or status.

Who – What category of customer are we dealing with?
What – What does the customer need to happen?
Where – Where and in what format does the customer need it to happen?
When – How soon does all of this need to be completed?

We don't neglect the 'Why' and the 'How'. The 'Why' is your SCO statement like the German automotive company's 'Joy' or the football team's 'Win the game'. The 'How' is the process of what you will now do to make the above happen.

If we were to look at an example of a man who's fence has fallen down in a storm and he is claiming on his insurance. We have decided that he has fallen into the category of 'Tech savvy, trustworthy customer' and realised that the real need is around getting the fence fixed, not the payout of the insurance. Why does this man need his fence replaced? The fence stops his children and pets running into the busy traffic and stops wild animals coming onto his property so really the fence in there as a symbol of security for this man. So we could conclude that his SCO is 'Security'.

We shouldn't be organising by department we should be organising by experience. Now of course a claims department who are fully aligned and rewarded on the speed and quality of their claims processing wouldn't look at the experience like this, why would they? Their goal is to process and close the claim as quickly and as cheaply as possible. This will involve assessments so they only have to pay out the bare minimum and to double check that the customer isn't lying to them by using deductible/excess payments from the customer to dissuade the customer from claiming at all, partial coverage of the damage to keep costs down, the list goes on. We can objectively look at this now and see that what they are doing isn't geared up towards the customer's success.

So using the template we would create a measurement that looks a little like this:
Who – Tech savvy, trustworthy customer
What – Full and secure fence
Where – Around the perimeter of their home
When – Within 24 hours of incident

So with this template, everyone in the process will be rewarded if and only if they deliver 'Security' to the customer, in this case for their tech savvy, trustworthy customers, security looks like a full and secure fence around the perimeter of their home within 24 hours of incident. Why will they do this? Well, because their job is now to deliver security to this category of customer. Remember 'Security' will mean different to different categories of customers, so will the KOI and therefore the solution the team will provide; this is moving away from process standardisation and towards experience personalisation.

How will you do this? Now that is the million-dollar question. Could you deliver this with your current claims department? Nope, so you would have to create a 'security experience team' that had many different skills, customer service, finance, IT, carpentry even. You know that they would all work together because they are all being rewarded for the delivery of that KOI not the success of their department. That KOI is very black and white, did it happen, yes or no? If it did you get your bonus, if it didn't you don't, simple as that.

I will add that if you also redefined where the process starts and finishes for the customer you might put in measures to make sure the fence never fell down in the first place thus eliminating the claim all together while still delivering a full and secure fence for the customer (as it never fell down). This is counter intuitive for a claims department because they need claims to come in so they can process them 'properly' to get their bonus.

However if you were in a 'Security Experience Team' it would be a very simple and intuitive solution to make precautions before the storm to stop damage from ever happening and thus preventing the loss of security for even a second for the customer. Building teams around the outcome that they are there to deliver allows a revolutionary and truly customer centric way of doing business.

We can also measure Interactions per Experience (IPE) to see how many touch points are necessary to deliver the SCO and work to reduce them. Many people think that you need to increase customer interaction but it has been proven that the higher the number of touchpoints in an experience the higher the level of dissatisfaction. We should be working to deliver the SCO in the lowest number of touchpoints possible. These measures shouldn't be department specific they should be experience specific. They are not internal measures of task and activity; they are external measures of success delivery.

It's not good enough in the 21st century to focus on process and experience improvement alone. We need to also turn our focus to 'Ecosystem Improvement'. It doesn't matter how fantastic your new customer experience is, if the environment that it will live in is not geared up to its survival and success it will fail.

The healthiest fish will soon die in the wrong water. You could do months of research, find the best Koi Carp breeder in the world, you could travel to them and purchase their prize fish, you could make sure it travels back home in the perfect conditions, you could have the best food and supplements ready for it's return but if you put it in salt water it will die.

When improving process and experience you need to understand the ecosystem, the habitat that the process and experience live within. If the habitat isn't conducive to the success of the experience it needs to change too. It's all about habits and habitats. The processes are the habits of the organisations and the mindsets, systems, targets, bonus structures, hierarchy and rules are the habitats that they live in. The Organisphere is the ecosystem, environment and habitat. The Organishere is the foundation for true customer centricity.

Chapter Seven - Customer Feedback

"Customer Experience is like sex, if you're good at it you don't need to ask how it went"

Originally I was going to mention how I felt about customer feedback in a few paragraphs, well, one thing led to another and… Welcome to Chapter Seven: Customer Feedback

Along the path to customer centricity most companies decide to enter the murky waters of customer feedback. The rationale behind this is that if we want to be truly customer centric we need to constantly try and gauge how happy our customers are, how satisfied they are with our service and if there is anything they think we could be doing better. On the surface this seems like sound reasoning however customer feedback surveys are probably the single least customer centric thing that any organisation can do.

Now I may have lost some of you at this point, at first it would seem crazy to abandon customer feedback surveys if you are on the journey towards true customer centricity but I shall explain why they are, at best, a complete waste of time.

Firstly, because of the way we have organised ourselves into hierarchical silos, a lot of what we do day to day is about proving to the person above us in the pyramid why we should still have a job and deserve our bonus; customer feedback surveys very often turn into another tool to help with this. When customer feedback is used in this way they are designed to highlight what a specific department or function is doing well, not to highlight the entire customer experience. Why would it? You are only getting rewarded for certain tasks and activities within your silo so why would you care about any other aspects of the customer experience? This is a very inside-out way of approaching feedback, not designed to help the customer, designed to help the company.

Traditional feedback surveys are flawed…extremely flawed. Net Promoter Score (NPS) Reichheld, Fred, Bain & Company and Satmetrix 2003 and different variations on the Customer Satisfaction Index (CSI) (ACSI) (CSAT)(NCSI)(UKCSI) along with online tools like GetFeedback, Client Heartbeat, CustomerSure, mycustomerfeedback.com, SurveyMonkey, Get Satisfaction, Hively and many many more. They are all basically a variation on the same theme of asking customers what they think and feel about your product, service or whole organisation. Basically, it doesn't matter what discipline or what platform you use to measure customer feedback, if you need to measure how well you are delivering customer experience through feedback surveys you are doing something wrong.

Ok, so let's go into some of the reasons that traditional feedback surveys aren't good enough.

They are self selecting. Are you the type of person that completes feedback surveys? If you have answered no, then there is someone out there who does that is influencing how businesses treat you, you are being represented by someone who is most likely nothing like you. If you answered yes then you are the minority, only a certain type of person completes feedback surveys on a regular basis and therefore business decisions are being made from the opinions of one very specific type of customer. Unless you can get every single customer to reply, the data is skewed and pretty much useless.

They are retrospective. They are mostly conducted after the fact, days, weeks and sometimes even months after the experience has happened. Memory and mood plays a big part in customer feedback if you were to ask me on a Monday morning how an experience 2 weeks ago was I might have a different answer than if you asked me on a Saturday night 1 month after the experience happened. Time and time again I get emails from hotels weeks after I have stayed with them asking me to do a survey on how the experience was, at my busiest I stayed in 5 different hotels in 2 weeks in 3 different continents. I have enough trouble remembering what country I'm supposed to be in next week let alone how good a hotel that I stayed in 4 weeks ago was.

Surveys are not broad enough. Most of the time, even if the question is about the experience as a whole, like the famous "How likely is it that you would recommend our company/product/service to a friend or colleague?" from NPS, they are asked after an interaction with one small part of the experience, usually with just one department. The question is in the context of the entire experience however only ever asked about or after an interaction that is a tiny part of the entire experience. For example, if a cable guy came and installed a new TV service for you and did a great job yet the whole process leading up to that was a nightmare and then you get a survey sent through about the installation process asking the famous NPS question, how do you answer this? The experience with the cable guy might rate as a 10 but the overall rating a 6, if you were to answer on the overall rating the cable guy would get a bad rating that maybe he didn't deserve but if you were to answer as a 10 the company would think they are doing better than they actually are. How is the customer expected to make the distinction? Either way you will get unreliable data.

The results are easily swayed. Some companies have taken the idea of rewarding employees for customer success and implemented it in the wrong way. They have decided that the measure of customer success is the feedback survey result. So employees will be rewarded for achieving good feedback survey results, this on the surface seems like a good idea however it isn't, and this is why. One reason is that the focus becomes improving the feedback score, not necessarily the actual customer experience so people try and find ways of getting the best feedback scores instead of finding ways to deliver the best customer experience.

Of course the employee knows that their bonus is dependent on the results of the survey and so will try and sway the customers response. "My dog's sick and we need to pay the vet bills…oh and by the way if you give me a bad rating I won't get my bonus and he might die." "My wife's car's break pads need replacing…oh and by the way if you give me a bad rating I won't get my bonus and I won't be able to replace them and she might crash and die." "Christmas is coming up and my kid wants a new bike…oh and by the way if you give me a bad rating I won't get my bonus and my kid wont get his bike and he might die…of sadness". All that these responses show you is which employees are the best at guilt tripping your customers.

A certain very large US carmaker stopped using NPS for this very reason. The sales people in their show rooms were spending more time explaining how their lives would fall apart if they received a bad rating than making sure their customers needs were met.

This meant that the company were receiving data that showed that as soon as their sales bonuses were largely influenced by customer feedback scores, their NPS score went through the roof and so decided to roll this out to other customer facing roles and by some miracle the same happened.

This company now thought they were doing very well and decided not to make any changes to their process or experience "if it's not broken, don't fix it", right? If you thought that you were at the top of the ladder you wouldn't take any steps to get higher would you? Now what this caused was a lot of annoyed customers that felt they were being coerced into giving high scores and an oblivious company who had no idea how upset their customers were so took no steps to change it.

Turning complex emotions into numbers is a very inexact science. It has been said time and time again that stories are the way to build customer affinity and make them feel a connection with your company. This should not only be extended to your organisations stories, actually listening to a customer's story is a very good way of determining how happy they are, not so you can then turn it into a number but so you can make things right for a customer or praise an employee for good work.

Interviewer: "On a scale of 1-10 with 1 being extremely impolite and 10 being extremely polite, how polite would you rate our engineer?"

Customer: "Oh I'm glad you asked, he was awful! He was rude and aggressive, he left muddy footprints on my carpet, he kept obnoxiously demanding drinks to which he would glug down and then belch to show his appreciation. He took phone calls in the middle of conversations with me on which he would curse and swear. He said various sexist comments and left an appalling mess everywhere that he went. To top it all of he didn't even complete the job before he made his excuses and left!"

Interviewer: "Oh no, how horrible…so…on a scale of 1-10 with 1 being extremely impolite and 10 being extremely polite, how polite would you rate our engineer?"

Nothing shows a customer how little you care about their actual situation faster than trying to reduce their feelings and emotions to a number that fits into a predetermined scale.

You only get extreme results. The majority of people tend to only leave feedback when they receive extremely good or extremely bad service. "Wow! The service I received at that restaurant yesterday was satisfactory, I must fill in a feedback survey and let them know." said no one ever.

The serial feedbackers will fill in feedback forms no matter what but the rest of the world only ever do this for the extremes or if there is a prize or incentive. With incentives to fill in feedback forms you get another type of person filling them in and again it is a very specific type of person.

I for instance am not one of these people, 10 minutes of my time in exchange for a 1 in 10,000 chance of winning the iPad I already have just isn't worth it for me. So even with the serial feedbacker's and the incentive feedbacker's input you still only have a very small percentage of your entire customer base's opinion.

If we're being honest most people just can't be bothered to fill in customer feedback surveys, feedback forms are boring, it feels like they don't make any difference and we're all just too busy to care.

You only get answers for the questions you ask. Feedback forms are mostly very assumptive, rather than explaining this I will take you through part of a survey that I received this week about a new house that we had built and moved into 9 months ago; long enough to get a feel for the house but long enough to forget lots too.

Part A: About your new home and the service you received from your builder/developer.

Question: Would you recommend your builder to a friend? Yes/No

Note: Now this is a tough one right off the bat. The guys that actually built the house were really helpful and bent over backwards to help us but dealing with the company itself was pretty bad. Also, recommending them to a friend, it really depends what type of friend, some friends I guess I would, other friends I definitely would not, so what do I answer?

Question: On a scale of 1 to 10 how likely would you be to recommend your builder to a friend?

Note: This kind of makes the question above pointless, asking a questions that requires a black or white answer only to then ask the same question again but with a graded answer is a waste of my time. It's like the question may as well be "You have said that you would be unlikely to recommend us to a friend, just how unlikely is that". It's like that weird kid at school who goes up to the popular girl and says "Will you go on a date with me?" and she answers "No" and the weird kid pushes on with "So, on a scale of 1-10 how unlikely is it?" and she replies "1" and the creepy kid says "So, you're saying there's a chance then?" It's just all a bit sad.

Question: Taking everything into account, overall how satisfied or dissatisfied were you with:

The quality of your new home? Very satisfied – Very dissatisfied

Note: Quality is a very subjective thing with different standards for different people, our standards are quite high for example. Does it mean build quality, the quality of the finish, the aesthetic quality, the quality of the appliances? It says take everything into account, well my answers would be different for every single aspect so I've now got to take an average, this isn't going to tell them anything useful.

Part B: About any problems there have been with your new home.

Question: Have you reported any problems to your builder since you moved in? Yes/No

Note: I'm being picky now, but yes we did, they know this, why do they need to ask me if we did?

Question: Was the number of problems in line with your expectations? Fewer/Same/Lower than expected

Note: We had a fair few things that needed to be put right, but we were fully expecting this because shortly after signing contracts there was a viral story about this company leaving people with lots of faults and problems with their new homes, so yes they met my expectations however my expectations were very low and shaped by unhappy customers. They will not get that information from this tick box question.

There are a load of questions about how satisfied we were with the repair work now, I'm not going to go through them all. We were very satisfied with the repair work but unsatisfied that it was needed; it's kind of like me asking "How satisfied were you with the apology I gave after punching you in the face" It really doesn't matter does it?

Question: Is there anything else you would like to add by way of explanation of your earlier responses? *1000 characters max*

Note: We really want to hear your opinions, unless you want to tell us in more than 1000 characters, then we don't care. Don't worry though we probably won't read this bit anyway.

Companies are using the data from these feedback initiatives to help make massive business decisions that is crazy. The data is so unreliable and skewed that the use of it is practically suicide.

Even though there are many reasons why feedback forms aren't useful the biggest point it this; are you trying to tell me that you don't know whether you are delivering a good customer experience or not? Surely you should know if you are delivering a good customer experience, shouldn't you?

Industry surveys should be taken with a pinch of salt too. For example, there is an airline called Ryanair. I can say with a high degree of certainty that 99.9% of the people reading this book are not Ryanair's desired category of customer. Many of you will have flown with Ryanair or heard stories of other people who have and will have the idea that they are one of the least customer centric companies in the world. That couldn't be further from the truth. Ryanair are possibly the world's most customer centric company and if you were their desired category of customer you would know this.

Arguably Ryanair have one category of customer and everything they do is aligned towards delivering success to them, them and only them. You could say that their ideal customer is one who will happily forego any glimmer of luxury in order to pay the lowest price possible, most likely not you or me. Possibly these are the only customers that Ryanair want, they don't want you or me to fly with them and in fact will actively discourage us from doing business with them. So I will ask you the question, the people that go and mystery shop for industry reviews, would they be Ryanair's desired category of customer? The answer would be no. Will they receive a good experience? The answer would be no. Do Ryanair care? The answer would no, because arguably they only care about the success of their customers and no matter if you have paid to be on a flight, if you do not fall into the category of customer that Ryanair want, you would not be their customer.

Anecdotally Ryanair understand their customers so much that a large percentage of their profits come from alcohol and gambling on the plane. They know that their ideal customers are traveling to a beach for a week or two of sun so they charge extra for baggage to force people to pack light, and subsequently have a staggeringly low lost bag rate, go figure! The SITA World Tracer Statistics for 2011 show a worldwide average of nine misplaced bags per 1,000 passengers, while Ryanair loses just 0.5 bags per 1,000. The study found that 53% of all lost baggage is a result of mishandled transfers. Rather worryingly, BA loses 16 bags per 1,000.

Recently Ryanair came bottom of a reader survey from 'Which? Magazine'. 'Which?' is an organisation that does consumer reviews on products and services and publishes them in various different mediums. Ryanair came out as the worst brand for customer service in the UK with 2 stars out of 5 producing an overall rating of 54% as a comparison British Airways scored 75%. It should be very obvious by now that the ideal British Airways passenger is not the ideal Ryanair passenger so the results are basically pointless. Ryanair responded to this in typical fashion. "We surveyed over three million passengers on the Ryanair website last night. Only two of them had ever heard of Which? and none of them had ever bought it or read it." Ryanair don't care about these industry reviews because they know that they are doing a good job, not for everybody, but for their preferred category of customer.

We can take all of this back to the football analogy. Let's imagine that 3 weeks ago you went to watch your local team play a match and all of a sudden you get an email from them asking you to fill out a questionnaire about your experience that was directly linked to your successful customer outcome.

Generic F.C.
Experience Questionnaire

In reference to the game you attended 3 weeks ago:

On a scale of 1-10:

Did we win?

1 – 2 – 3 – 4 – 5 – 6 – 7 – 8 – 9 – 10

On a scale of 1-10, did we win? If you received something like that how would that make you feel? What would it make you think? You might think something like "Do they not know if they won or not? Surely they should know this!" You could try and make the questionnaire a touch smarter and ask questions like:

On a scale of 1-10 how satisfied were you with the amount of passes we made?

On a scale of 1-10 how pleased were you with the amount of tackles we made?

On a scale of 1-10 satisfied were you with the amount of shots at goal we took?

You might look at these from a business mind set and think "Well, yes these would be better questions because we already know if we won or not so those questions would provide more useful data" however from a customer mind set you would think "Why are they asking me this? That's what they have managers and coaches for. They review the performance see what went well and what could be improved"

The whole theme of this is; if you know the true SCO that needs to be delivered for your customer and the core things that need to be done to deliver it; you don't need to ask your customers if they happened or not, you should already know.

The following is a quote taken directly from and article in The Telegraph online newspaper about the book 'The Footballer's Guide to the Modern Game'

"I have never read fans' forums. Ever. Totally pointless. I know more than any fan in the country about how football should be played and what it takes to win matches, so I am not going to read anything that they say about what happened in a match or how I or my team-mates are playing. I know when I've played well and what went right, and I know when I've played badly and what went wrong. If I need help, I'll ask my coaches. That's what they're paid for."

Another point to draw from this is that in football, the managers and coaches are reviewing the game at every point, every pass, every tackle, every run, every shot. If things aren't quite going to plan they will make changes in the process there and then. They wouldn't start a game with a specific tactic, play the game, see things are going badly, decide to keep the tactics because that's what has already been communicated to the players, lose the game, send out a feedback letter, look at the feedback, put forward a case for tactic change, get approved, make changes for the next game. If a manager or a coach of a football team did that then they would get fired for sure. What they do is make changes as they go, if things aren't on track to achieve the win they will do things differently. Not in the next game, not at the next strategy review, right now.

It is exactly like that in business. The inside-out companies will communicate a strategy or process procedures, watch them run, see that they are going badly but do nothing because these are the rules and procedures, send out feedback forms to their customers, get feedback that things have been going badly (remember they already know this) put a case together for the next strategy review (usually yearly) present it, get it accepted or declined and carry on from there. This is just not fast enough in the 21st century. In Outside-In companies, the SCO is their strategy, so they do whatever it takes, in the moment to deliver it. Employees become empowered to make decisions on behalf of the business as long at they will help the customer achieve his or her SCO.

In inside-out companies all process looks the same but the customer outcomes are varied and unpredictable, in outside-in companies no two processes look the same but the outcomes are consistently and successfully delivered. You will find that the best football teams will play differently every single time however they will achieve the successful outcome more regularly and consistently than the other teams.

Customer Experience is like sex, if you're good at it you don't need to ask how it went. If you need to ask, you have your answer. Just like in sex the people who are good at it monitor the entire experience in real time and if things aren't going right they change their approach. They don't just carry on doing things in the same way then ask at the end what they could do better next time, in this day and age there might not be a next time. It is important to understand what a successful outcome is for your customer and do whatever it takes to deliver it. As long as you know what a successful customer outcome is and the things to measure it by, as long as you achieve it and those measures, you know that you have done a good job. No need to ask.

It's exactly the same in football and truly customer centric companies. In the moment if its not going too well you can change things, try different tactics, make substitutions...that analogy is just for football and business...unless that's your sort of thing. You shouldn't wait until its gone badly to change the things that you do. You should change things while you're in the process to make sure it goes well and to guarantee that you deliver a successful customer outcome.

Chapter Eight - Kick Off

"The future is not constrained by our conditions it's defined by our decisions"

When teams are organised to deliver SCO's and told that their job is to deliver SCO's the entire organisation changes. No matter who you are in the organisation you become empowered to use your brilliance and creativity to help achieve customer success instead of having everything that makes you you marginalised and suppressed so you can complete your tasks and activities in the most efficient manner.

Everyone has the potential to be brilliant however if we force everyone to do everything in the same way only a few people get to really shine. 5 + 5 equals 10, however so does 3 + 7, so does 1 + 9, so does 12 – 2. There are many different ways of getting to the same result and we are killing our employees spirit by telling them that there is only one way and they have to do it that way or else. As long as we know what the result needs to be we should allow our employees the freedom to get there by themselves; instead of controlling their daily tasks and activities we should be supporting them to make the right decisions to deliver customer success.

Why don't we do that now? It's all down to trust, we don't trust our employees. You need to ask the question "Who is going out and hiring all of these untrustworthy people?" How can you expect your staff to deliver outstanding customer experiences when you don't trust them to do so? A lot of this mistrust comes down to our current departmental mindsets where we see other departments as enemies. Have you ever stopped to think just how much money it costs your organisation every year to not trust your employees?

When you organise your foundations for customer centricity things will be different but it doesn't have to be a big drama, in your experience teams people will still have specialties, just like in a football team. There will always be people who are better at working with technology, there will always be people who are better at working with numbers, there will always be people who are better at dealing with customers, but over time as they all work together to deliver the same goal, they will learn from each other and in time you will organically develop a multi-skilled workforce.

You will meet resistance, of course you will. There will always be people who resent being pushed aside when they get told that the customer is more important than them. There will always be people who have done things the same way for their entire careers that will not want to adopt a new way of thinking. There will always be people who are emotionally resistant to change.

You will meet people who want to join the revolution, of course you will. There will always be people who have open ears and minds to new ideas, there will always be people who have been looking for a different way but just hadn't found it yet. Either way, below is a great diagram showing the efficacy of focusing on customer experience. This was created and first shown to me by a friend, a colleague of mine called Mark Barnett, I've tweaked it just a touch but it is still most definitely his creation.

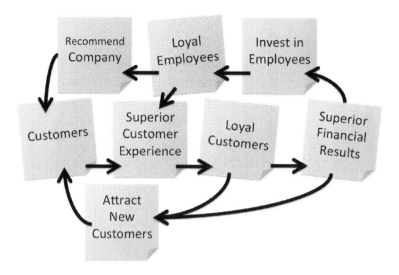

I'll try and explain it and do it as much justice as I can. You start with customers, always start with customers. You then have a choice; sub par or superior customer experience, if you chose the latter you will naturally nurture loyal customers. Loyal customers will help on two fronts, attracting new customers who you can give your amazing experience to and providing superior financial results.

With this money you can attract more customers who can be given your astounding experience and very importantly you can invest in your employees. Investing in your employees makes them feel valued and rewarded, many prefer investment in their personal and career growth over financial bonuses. Investing in employees doesn't just mean your current employees it means that you can pay a higher wage and give better benefits thus attracting the best people, take all of that into account and you will have a workforce who are ready and enthused to give your customers the best service in the world. This will create a very loyal workforce.

Do you want to work for someone who pays less, doesn't invest in you and controls every aspect of your day being constantly told "Don't think just do" or do you want to work for someone that pays the most, heavily invests in you and allows you the freedom and support to do the right thing? The question needs no answer.

You organically garner a workforce who will do whatever it takes to stay with you, and if their job is based on delivering SCO's they will make sure that is their focus because they want to remain employed by such a magnificent employer. When friends and acquaintances ask your employees "Where do you work?" Do they hang their head, mumble and mutter or to they stand tall and proudly shout? Of course if your workforce are shouting about how great you are they will draw new customers too and that's right you can then feed these new customers into your new mind-blowing customer experience and the rest is history.

Depending on commitment and enthusiasm within your organisation you can start big or small. In corporate-land (Not as fun as Disney Land) we spend a worrying portion of our time practicing the art of ESM (Ego Satisfaction Management) with our colleagues. Do remember that because of the way we draw the pyramid there is a clear message to the hierarchy that if your little box is drawn higher than someone else's little box then you are a better, more important, more influential person than them, of course you are, you are closer to the most important person in the company, the CEO, right? If your inferiors don't act as if this is the situation at every interaction it's your job to remind them, of course it is, you need to keep control, right?

If you run around shouting and preaching about the ideas in the book people aren't necessarily going to respond positively, how could a mere underling know more than someone who's little box is drawn above them? It couldn't happen, right? The best way is to start small and get success. These people will then come to you and ask you to tell them how you did it "How did you achieve so much, in such a short amount of time, for such little cost?" and then you can tell them. If you go and tell them how things should be done, they feel stupid and they will dismiss it but if they come and ask you they feel like the smart one who has sourced a paradigm shifting new way of doing things.

Something as little as changing how you represent your organisation diagrammatically is a good enough start to help change mindsets and how people see the organisational ecosystem that your customer experience lives within.

The first step is in understanding your organisation's true customer centric maturity, understanding the mindsets you will be working with and how you should be talking to them. You wouldn't talk to your grandmother the same way as you would talk to a friend in a bar; to get the best results make sure you are talking to them in their language.

Unfortunately this isn't something that many outside consultancies can help with (apart from the BP Group and it's partners) because the majority of them are stuck in the past trying to sell you solutions based on the old pyramidal way of thinking. I have no doubt that some of you will read this and think "Oh my god! This is great, a new way of doing things from a new breed of customer experience experts, we need to do this, it makes perfect sense…I wonder if Accenture can do it for us" If this is you please either re-read or burn the book now, you have learned nothing.

You just kind of need to get stuck in for yourself, even if you were to engage the BP Group to help with this we would still need the involvement of the people on the ground in your organisation; no one knows your business like the people doing the work day in day out. Unlike traditional consultancies we get in, transfer knowledge and get out. It's how we have managed to work with and learn from so many companies, we let you deliver the transformation for yourself with a little bit of hand holding if desired. Our goal isn't to create a consultancy dependency like 99% of the other consultancies. Our goal is your success.

Like a great bottle of scotch, or an outdated management methodology all good things must come to an end but with the end of this book comes an exciting beginning, the start of your journey to true customer centricity. Whether you have taken a little or a lot from this book you will never look at business in quite the same way again. As it's a short book you should feel confident to read it again, pass it around and share it with people.

Some of you will be thinking that you can't make changes or that your company is too unique and that this is too big of a change for you. If that's how you think then you are right, if your brain automatically jumps to the reasons why you're not going to do something over ways you can start to do something you need to have a long hard look in the mirror. The majority of these ideas are about mindset and you have to get yours right before trying to do anything or influencing anyone.

All of the things that you think stand in your way are just the conditions you are working within. The future is not constrained by our conditions it's defined by our decisions. There is a long list of things you have no control over in your organisation but how you think and the decisions you make are not on it and never will be. The only things in life that you have 100% control over is how you think and the decisions you make. You can make any decision you want, the only thing stopping you is fear and fear is a decision. If you believe you can do it, you will be able to do it and belief is a decision. Any organisation can become truly customer centric because true customer centricity is a decision.

Bibliography

Asghar, R. (2014). *One Company's Success Story: Who Needs A CEO Anyway?*. [online] Forbes. Available at: http://www.forbes.com/sites/robasghar/2014/03/14/one-companys-success-story-who-needs-a-ceo-anyway/ [Accessed 30 Dec. 2014].

Bailey, M. (2014). *The Secret Footballer: 'Players don't care what fans think' - Telegraph*. [online] Telegraph.co.uk. Available at: http://www.telegraph.co.uk/men/active/11205600/The-Secret-Footballer-Players-dont-care-what-fans-think.html [Accessed 30 Dec. 2014].

Barnett, M. (2013). *Virtuous Growth Spiral*.

Biography.com, (2014). *Jeff Bezos Biography*. [online] Available at: http://www.biography.com/people/jeff-bezos-9542209 [Accessed 30 Dec. 2014].

Biography.com, (2014). *Steve Jobs Biography*. [online] Available at: http://www.biography.com/people/steve-jobs-9354805 [Accessed 30 Dec. 2014].

Client Heartbeat, (2014). *Client Heartbeat: Customer Satisfaction Software Tool*. [online] Available at: http://www.clientheartbeat.com [Accessed 30 Dec. 2014].

Cornet, M. (2011). *Organizational Charts | Bonkers World*. [online] Bonkersworld.net. Available at: http://www.bonkersworld.net/organizational-charts/ [Accessed 30 Dec. 2014].

Customersure.com, (2014). *Customer Feedback and Follow-Up Software*. [online] Available at: http://www.customersure.com [Accessed 30 Dec. 2014].

Deming.org, (2014). *THE THEORIES AND TEACHINGS OF DR. W. EDWARDS DEMING ARE NOTHING SHORT OF TRANSFORMATIONAL IN SPIRIT AND IN PRACTICE.*. [online] Available at: https://deming.org/theman/theories [Accessed 30 Dec. 2014].

DevOpsGuys, (2013). *DevOps, Adam Smith and the legend of the Generalist*. [online] Available at: http://blog.devopsguys.com/2013/09/24/devops-adam-smith-and-the-legend-of-the-generalist/ [Accessed 30 Dec. 2014].

Education Portal, (2014). *What Is a Flat Structure in an Organization? - Definition, Advantages & Disadvantages | Education Portal*. [online] Available at: http://education-portal.com/academy/lesson/what-is-a-flat-structure-in-an-organization-definition-advantages-disadvantages.html [Accessed 30 Dec. 2014].

Forbes, (2013). *Richard Branson Reveals His Customer Service Secrets.* [video] Available at: https://www.youtube.com/watch?v=Fy4lYDN1gz4 [Accessed 30 Dec. 2014].

Gallo, C. (2012). *How the Ritz-Carlton Inspired the Apple Store [video].* [online] Forbes. Available at: http://www.forbes.com/sites/carminegallo/2012/04/10/how-the-ritz-carlton-inspired-the-apple-store-video/ [Accessed 30 Dec. 2014].

Gartner.com, (2014). *Technology Research | Gartner Inc..* [online] Available at: http://www.gartner.com/technology/home.jsp [Accessed 30 Dec. 2014].

Get Satisfaction, (2014). *Get Satisfaction - Customer Communities For Social Support, Social Marketing & Customer Feedback.* [online] Available at: http://www.getsatisfaction.com [Accessed 30 Dec. 2014].

GetFeedback, (2014). *GetFeedback - Online Surveys Re-Imagined.* [online] Available at: http://www.getfeedback.com [Accessed 30 Dec. 2014].

Global-integration, (2014). *What is a matrix organization structure?.* [online] Available at: http://www.global-integration.com/matrix-management/matrix-structure/matrix-organization-structure/ [Accessed 30 Dec. 2014].

Hively.com, (2014). *HIVELY.COM.* [online] Available at: http://www.hively.com [Accessed 30 Dec. 2014].

Instituteofcustomerservice.com, (2014). *Institute of Customer Service - Home.* [online] Available at: http://www.instituteofcustomerservice.com [Accessed 30 Dec. 2014].

Mspartner.microsoft.com, (2014). *Customer Satisfaction Index.* [online] Available at: https://mspartner.microsoft.com/en/us/pages/sales%20and%20marketing/customer-satisfaction-index.aspx [Accessed 30 Dec. 2014].

Mycustomerfeedback.com, (2014). *Customer Complaints & Feedback Management Software.* [online] Available at: http://www.mycustomerfeedback.com [Accessed 30 Dec. 2014].

Ncsiuk.com, (2014). *NCSI.* [online] Available at: http://ncsiuk.com [Accessed 30 Dec. 2014].

Netpromoter.com, (2014). *The Net Promoter Score and System - Net Promoter Community.* [online] Available at: http://www.netpromoter.com/why-net-promoter/know/ [Accessed 30 Dec. 2014].

Robinson, S. (2010). *RSA - Changing Paradigms.* [online] Thersa.org. Available at: http://www.thersa.org/events/video/archive/sir-ken-robinson [Accessed 30 Dec. 2014].

Rolls-royce.com, (2014). *Rolls-Royce*. [online] Available at: http://www.rolls-royce.com [Accessed 30 Dec. 2014].

Rubiks, (2014). *Rubiks History*. [online] Available at: http://uk.rubiks.com/history [Accessed 30 Dec. 2014].

Ryanair, (2014). *Cheap Flights | Cheap Flights to Europe | Ryanair*. [online] Available at: http://www.ryanair.com [Accessed 30 Dec. 2014].
Secret Footballer, (n.d.). *The Secret Footballer's guide to the modern game.*

Smith, O. (2013). *Ryanair 'worst' brand for customer service - Telegraph*. [online] Telegraph.co.uk. Available at: http://www.telegraph.co.uk/travel/travelnews/10319838/Ryanair-worst-brand-for-customer-service.html [Accessed 30 Dec. 2014].

Sonny, J. (2013). *The 10 Most Successful People With ADHD*. [online] Elite Daily. Available at: http://elitedaily.com/money/10-successful-people-adhd/ [Accessed 30 Dec. 2014].

Surveymonkey.com, (2014). *SurveyMonkey: Free online survey software & questionnaire tool*. [online] Available at: http://www.surveymonkey.com [Accessed 30 Dec. 2014].

Systems, V. (2014). *Customer Experience and VOC Excellence @ Gartner 360 Summit*. [online] Blog.verint.com. Available at: http://blog.verint.com/blog/bid/316909/Customer-Experience-and-VOC-Excellence-Gartner-360-Summit [Accessed 30 Dec. 2014].

Theacsi.org, (2014). *The American Customer Satisfaction Index*. [online] Available at: http://www.theacsi.org [Accessed 30 Dec. 2014].

Which.co.uk, (2014). *Reviews and expert advice from Which?*. [online] Available at: http://www.which.co.uk [Accessed 30 Dec. 2014].

www.Budgetairlinewatch.com, (2014). *Ryanair baggage in the news: low lost luggage statistics and EU cabin bag ruling*. [online] Available at: http://budgetairlinewatch.com/?p=722 [Accessed 30 Dec. 2014].

Printed in Great Britain
by Amazon